Note to Parents and Teachers

The READING ABOUT: STARTERS series introduces key science vocabulary to young children while encouraging them to discover and understand the world around them. The series works as a set of graded readers in three levels.

LEVEL 1: BEGINNING TO READ follows guidelines set out in the National Curriculum for Year 1. These books can be read alone or as part of guided or group reading. Each book has three sections:

- Information pages that introduce new words. These key words appear in bold throughout the book for easy recognition.
- A lively story that recalls this vocabulary and encourages children to use these words when they talk and write.
- A quiz and word search ask children to look back and recall what they have read.

SOFT TOYS, TOUGH TOYS looks at SORTING MATERIALS. Below are some activities related to the questions on the information spreads that parents, carers and teachers can use to discuss and develop further ideas and concepts:

p. 5 *Why is metal a good material for a toy crane?* Ask children to handle metal toys. Ask about unsuitable alternatives, e.g. spade made from bendy or squishy material.

p. 7 *Why is plastic a good material for baby toys?* Exploring safety issues; contrast with unsuitable materials, e.g. sharp or heavy objects, materials that cannot be easily cleaned, small parts that may be swallowed.

p. 9 *Which of your toys are cuddly?* Exploring how materials feel. Could be extended with a blindfold test where children use touch, smell and hearing to identify materials.

p. 11 *What things around your house are made of wood?* Ask children to think about how common materials are used and to suggest suitable uses for them.

p. 13 *What else can you squash into different shapes?* Exploring maleable and rigid materials and the difference in materials when wet and dry e.g. clay, sand, paper.

p. 15 *Try different ways of folding paper into a dart.* Or other simple origami models.

p. 17 *Which ball do you think bounces best?* Compare elasticity of different materials.

p. 19 *Why is plastic a good material for a juice bottle?* Looking at transparency and safety issues re: glass. Ask children why wood and metal are not as suitable.

p. 21 *Which of your clothes and toys are waterproof?* Could extend to other waterproof items and materials, e.g. diver's wetsuit, roof and windows, baths/pools.

ADVISORY TEAM

Educational Consultant
Andrea Bright – Science Co-ordinator, Trafalgar Junior School, Twickenham

Literacy Consultant
Jackie Holderness – former Senior Lecturer in Primary Education, Westminster Institute, Oxford Brookes University

Series Consultants
Anne Fussell – Early Years Teacher and University Tutor, Westminster College, Oxford Brookes University

David Fussell – C.Chem., FRSC

CONTENTS

© Aladdin Books Ltd 2004

Designed and produced by
Aladdin Books Ltd
2/3 Fitzroy Mews
London W1T 6DF

First published in
Great Britain in 2004 by
Franklin Watts
96 Leonard Street
London EC2A 4XD

A catalogue record for this book is available from the British Library.

ISBN 0 7496 5592 5

Printed in UAE

All rights reserved

Editor: Jim Pipe

Design: Flick, Book Design and Graphics

Picture research:
Brian Hunter Smart

Thanks to:
• The pupils of Trafalgar Infants School, Twickenham for appearing as models in this book.
• Lynne Thompson for helping to organise the photoshoots.
• The pupils and teachers of Trafalgar Junior School, Twickenham and St. Nicholas C.E. Infant School, Wallingford, for testing the sample books.

Photocredits:
l-left, r-right, b-bottom, t-top, c-centre, m-middle
All photos supplied by PBD except for:
Front cover tl & tm, 8tl, 14br, 17mr, 31ml, 32tr — Photodisc.
Front cover tr, 6t, 7 both, 11l, 12, 13 both, 16mr, 17b, 19 both, 21bl, 21br, 22br, 31mr, 32mlt, 32bl, 32mrb — Jim Pipe. 2ml, 5bl, 16tl, 32mlb — Corbis. 5mr, 6br, 11r, 32tl, 32mrt — Flick Smith. 9 — Brand X Pictures. 18l — Digital Vision. 22bl — Dave Sinclair/Natural Resources Canada (www.nrcan.gc.ca). 23tr, 32br — Ken Hammond/USDA. 23ml — USDA. 23br — Select Pictures.

SORTING MATERIALS
Tough Toys, Soft Toys

by Sally Hewitt

Aladdin/Watts

London • Sydney

Things are made of **materials**.

Metal is a **material**.

This crane is made of **tough metal**.

Some things need to be **tough**.
You swing from **metal** bars.
You play with a **metal** car.
You dig with a **metal** spade.

Bars

Car

Spade

• Why is metal a good material for a toy crane?

Toys made of **plastic**
are **smooth** and **light**.
Plastic is easy to wash.
It is very difficult to break.

6

Baby toys are often made of **plastic**.
Babies throw their toys.
They put toys in their mouths!

• Why is plastic a good material for baby toys?

Soft toys are made to be **cuddly**.
They feel **soft** and **squishy**.

A wooden horse is not
made to be **cuddly**!

8

A **cuddly** toy is made of **soft cloth**.

It is stuffed with **soft, squishy** material.

• Which of your toys are cuddly?

Toy bricks are made of **wood**.
They feel smooth and **hard**.
Wooden bricks don't break
when they fall down!

10

Tools are used to carve **wood**
into different **shapes**.
A saw cuts the **wood**.
A chisel **shapes** it. Watch out, it's sharp!
Sandpaper makes it smooth.

Chisel

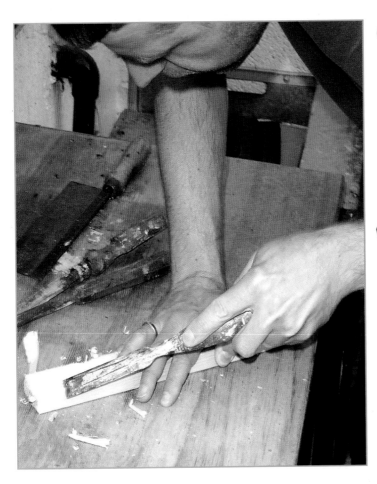

• What things around your house are made of wood?

Clay is a kind of mud.

It is good for making models.

Wet clay feels soft and squishy.

You can squash, press, bend and roll **wet clay** into different shapes.

Wet clay is soft.
Dry clay is hard.

You can **dry** a **clay** model and paint it.

Paper is thin and light.
You can **tear paper**.

You can **cut** it with
scissors to make
different shapes.

14

You can **fold** paper to make different shapes too.

A **paper** dart is very light.
It flies through the air.

• *Try different ways of folding paper into a dart.*

Rubber is squashy.

If you drop it, it **bounces**.

A basketball is made of **rubber**.

Balloons are made of rubber too. You can **stretch** them to make funny shapes.

16

Balls are made of different materials.
A basketball is made of **rubber**.
A football is made of leather.
A beach **ball** is made of plastic.

• Which ball do you think bounces best?

Glass is **transparent**.
You can see through **glass**.
Windows are made of **glass**.
You can see toys through a
toy shop window.

18

Glass breaks easily.
A plastic bottle is tough and difficult
to **break**. It is **transparent** too.

You can see the orange
juice in the plastic bottle.

• Why is plastic a good material for a juice bottle?

A playground must be a **safe** place
for children to play.
The slide is made of smooth metal.
The ground is made of rubber.
You will bounce if you fall on it!

Water toys are **waterproof**.
Water does not **soak** into them.

Water can **soak** into your clothes,
but plastic boots are **waterproof**.

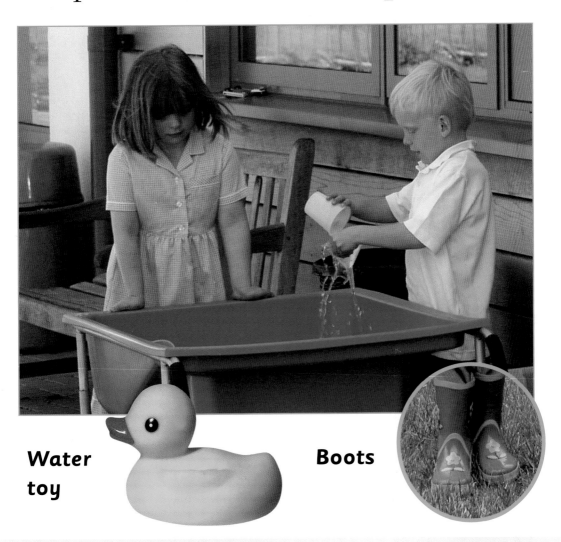

**Water
toy**

Boots

• Which of your clothes and toys are waterproof?

Toys can be made of wood, metal, cloth or plastics.

Wood comes from the trunks and branches of **trees**.

Metal is dug up from the ground.

22

Cloth can be made from **wool** or **cotton**.

Wool comes from sheep.

Cotton comes from a plant.

Plastics are made in lots of different ways.

· What materials are the toys in this book made of?

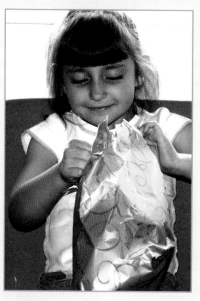

Now read the story of **Rita's Birthday.** Look out for words about **materials**.

Rita's friends have come to her birthday party.

Rita loves her presents.

"I can fly the **paper** kite!" she says. "I can **bounce** the **ball**. I can **cuddle** the **soft** puppy."

"There's a present for you all in the **plastic** tub," says Mum. "Feel it first. Can you guess what it is?"

I can feel something **tough** and **hard**," says Raj. "It's made of **metal**. It's got wheels."

Everyone shouts, "It's a truck!"

It is a truck!

Rosie puts her hand in the tub.
"I can feel crinkly **paper**.
I can feel the **smooth plastic** tub."

Rosie looks sad.
"I can't feel a
present," she says.

"Let me try!"
says Rita.

She feels in the
bottom of the tub.

"I can feel something round and squashy. I think it's made of **rubber!**" says Rita.

Rosie smiles.
It's a **bouncy rubber ball!**

Will finds something **soft** and **squishy**. It's made of **cloth**. It's a teddy!

Will doesn't want
a **cuddly** teddy.

So Will and Rosie
swap toys.

Will plays with the **rubber** ball.
Rosie **cuddles** the **soft** teddy.

Gemma puts both hands
in the **plastic** tub.

"I can feel something
round. It's **smooth**.
It's very **light**. It's made
of **plastic**," she says.

"It's a plate!"
guesses Rosie.

"No, silly,
it's a Frisbee!"
laughs Gemma.

"I've got something **soft** and **smooth** and very cold!" says Mum.

"Ice cream!" shout the children. "My favourite!" says Rita.

Write labels with the words: **metal** • **paper** • **wood** • **plastic** • **rubber** • **cloth**.

What are your toys made of? Put them next to the right label.

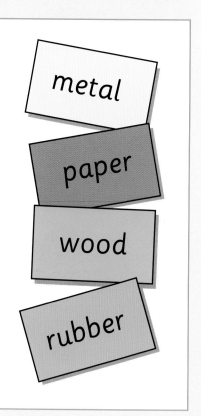

QUIZ

What **material** is this crane made of?

Answer on page 4

Who plays with
this **plastic** toy?

Answer on page 7

Does **dry clay** feel **soft** or **hard**?

Answer on page 13

Why are windows
made of **glass**?

Answer on page 18

Did you know the answers? Give yourself a

Do you remember these **materials** words?
Well done! Can you remember any more?

metal
page 5

plastic
page 6

cloth
page 9

wood
page 11

clay
page 12

paper
page 14

rubber
page 16

glass
page 19

waterproof
page 21

wool
page 23